Moments and Time

Ricardo Marquez

Presentation by *BookLeaf Publishing*

Web: www.bookleafpub.com

E-mail: info@bookleafpub.com

ISBN: 9789357211529

First edition 2023

PREFACE

Moments and Time is a collection of poems written in the later months of 2022. A time of self-exploration and destruction. A group of moments driven forward by time and self-surrender. Like Time, these poems progress, never revisiting the moments of the past. Instead, Ricardo explores the dark places within society and his mind. He destroys pieces of himself along the way—a poetic catharsis for the average person dealing with the dark elements of the human condition.

Chairs

An empty chair sits alone beside me.
Aged oak and spiraling spindles stained brown.
A perfect arrangement of nothing now sturdy,
On the cold, damp ground.

I'm Jealous.

We don't need chairs,
not like they need us.
We exist without any reason.
Chairs exist solely for a reason.

For us.

To me, to me chairs are sacred,
They are purposeful in a world that is purposeless.
Stubborn reminders of our sorry existence.
Testimony to our desperate attempts
of outrunning the darkness behind every sunset.

Yet,
Chairs are just chairs.
Merely judged on what they provide.
And like that,
I think we are chairs too.
Just with the emptiness inside.

A Blur

I'm living in a blur
The type that bends the mind
And time.
One by one, then
Again once more.
Till they're one.
And then, I'm no more.

I'm living in a blur
The type where everything floats
And I sink, and I cope.
But the blur gets blurrier still
And I fall further in
To myself.
Until blurry is all that's left.
Then, living in a blur
Is all that makes sense.

Self-Explore

Am I what I believe or,
Do I believe the lies?
The ones that make me feel
like you and I
are the same.

Am I what I believe or,
am I unbelievable,
paradoxical, and lame.

Do I believe enough?
Am I
Enough?
Enough.

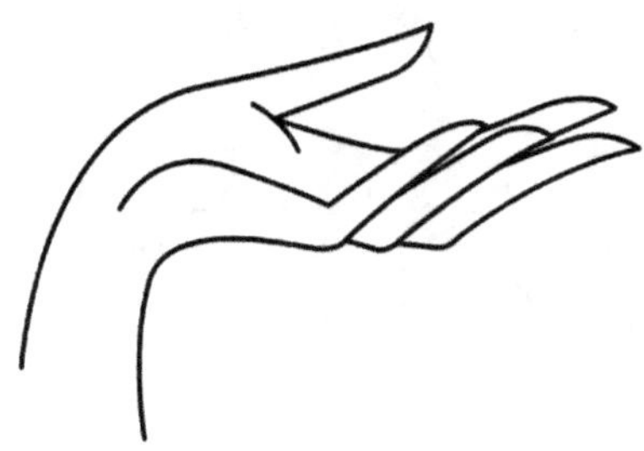

Boo-Hoo

Boo-Hoo, stop crying
No one hears you
No one cares to
so stop crying, and saying
that life's unfair.
Blaming the world
for the scars that bare
you and your skin.

Boo-Hoo, Its true,
What are you going to do?
Nothing, so Boo-Hoo poor you
No one hears you crying,
No one cares but you.
Boo-Hoo

I've Never Tried

I've never tried
a beer or two
to treat the angst.
The burden, the flame
Living in the depths
of my soul.
A fuse,
waiting to ignite.
Explode,
and burn the world.

It rumbles when I move
Sparking when near you,
or anyone my heart loves true.

Maybe I'll try that beer, or two.
To undo myself for you.
Then, the world would burn
and the sky would darken too.
And you would see me truly,
like the way I see you.
So maybe yes, I'll take that beer or two.

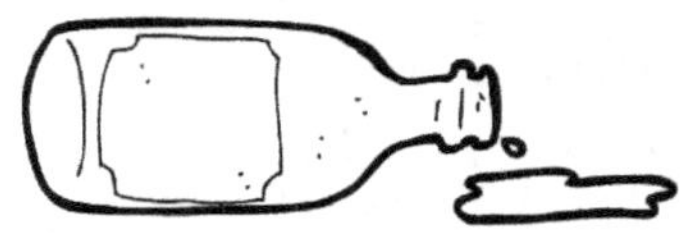

Nothing at all

I have everything and nothing
at all.

Balancing chaos and peace
in winter, spring, summer, and fall.
Seasonal changes, changing nothing
at all.
I have everything to look forward to
and nothing to look back upon.

Nothing at all.

Traumas that trickle through time
tracing me forward until I find
A reason to close my withering mind
and silence the voices speaking from
inside.

It's nothing, life. Just a price and place
with everything and nothing
at all.
Nothing to offer.
Nothing to take.
Nothing at all.

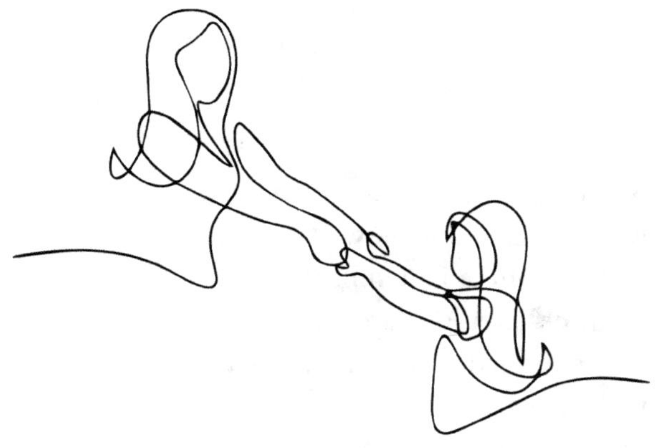

a truth

we built towers and countries
with power and money.
made meaning in nothing
while children go hungry.
own dogs and cats, and busy ourselves
with studies.
just to brag later online to people who
are too, running.

Blurry nights weekly,
in bars filled with
people and ghosts
who all just want to feel something real
have someone close
enough to touch their lonely hearts
and unlearned souls

if only the schools we built
and the libraries we filled
gave us the answers to guide us
to a world, we were promised
a world without fear

then we would know a truth;
that nothing is forever

and that nothing is you
cherish everything and everyone
because they are nothing too.
and nothing is forever, a truth.

Awareness

I'm mindful almost always

It exhausts me.

My mind is always here

even as it costs me

my peace. My turn

to be mindless

is something I chase

something I yearn

An emptiness that refills me

An emptiness that's safe, like home.

I'm mindful now, its midnight too

Both of which fill my mind with you.

I'm mindful almost always

But today my mind is twice as full

costing me tomorrows peace

I'd purge it if I could.

But I cannot purge what does not exist,

and I cannot outrun my thoughts

So alone with them, I sit.

Aware of the hole deep within

and all I go without.

Awareness, a sin.

A laugh

A burial would be nice,
lied to one last time
about the importance
and impact
of untapped potential left
inside my corpse
and rotting mind.
Lies, lies, and more lies
Disguised as love letters
from ignorant people
silently celebrating my demise.
People are funny when they act
so a burial would be nice, just for laughs.

Places

I've been to places
both far and near
places stamped with faces
far away from here.
I've been to places
I can't share
Places so sacred
using words is unfair.
I've been to these places
one after the next
looking for new places
to travel to next
All of these places are painted the same
hues of vibrant colors
Colors I cannot name
I've been to places
more often than most
But no place is like
the place I call home.

The Hummingbird Sings

Do you know why
the Hummingbird sings?
Amongst you, they roam,
Rarely unseen.
Keeping you close,
like the breath
that you breathe.

They work like magic
for the fools who believe
that the goal of our lives
mean seizing the day most passionately.

Again, A life full of passion
Is worth spending time to achieve.
So then, with passion untamed
these fools suffer and bleed
Hearts branded with scars, yet
still with life they proceed.

Like magic for fools
these hummingbirds sing
But only if you're lucky
and live foolishly free
will you hear the hummingbird sing.

Magic for fools is what
the hummingbirds' sing
A song for those who live passionately
in a world with no passion to live

Resistance

How is it, that tearing force?
Ripping you at the seams,
until you're helplessly torn
to bits
and pieces
of which make you
or at least
did
How is it?
Resistance.

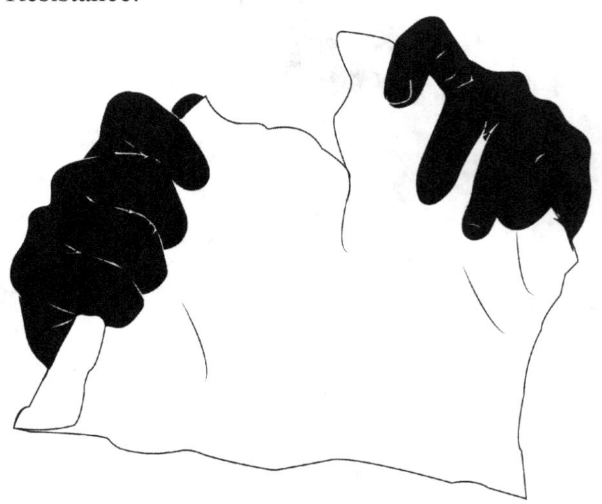

Thursday afternoon

A Thursday afternoon
and I'm alone.
The sun is shining down
on the world.
On my soul.
I'm unresolved
and afraid.
This Thursday afternoon is
turning me into someone
I ain't.
Someone I hate.

Fighter

I am a fighter who seldom bleeds
onto others around me.
Instead, I pump that blood
back inside of me.
To keep me fighting
and bleeding.
Surviving and
barely breathing.

I am a fighter who throws fire
missiles that don't misfire.
I'll fight till I die, and then some after.
Until I tire, and sometimes I do
tire.

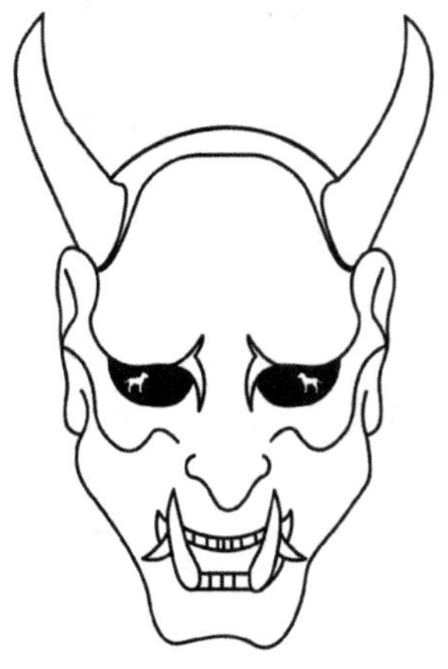

good betrayal

I don't want to betray those I love
But I do; in the past, I have too.
I've broken the trust of more than a few.
Who knew?
That Id burden the world more than
I'd wished to.
But now I understand that I was born
into betrayal too.
A habit I learned watching others
breaking their promises too.
I didn't know it was something.
I wasn't supposed to do it.
Breaking things hurts,
but they change things too.
That's good a betrayal can do.

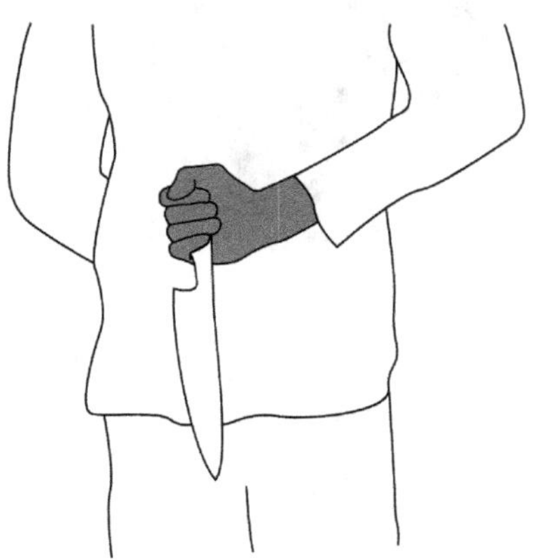

Self-Sabotage

I ruin everything, including myself
I build mountains of possibilities
and just yesterday I fell
off and away
from heaven to hell
because I am undeserving
of the love up there.

god chose my friend

Why did he take you instead?
A beautiful girl once glowing
now dead.

In the backseat of an 03 Chevy
with two poor souls at the head
Not like you, darkness was their friend.

Maybe that's why he took you instead?
cause you shined too bright
with that light that you led

The world is consumed in darkness
and you light lit up this mess
Something he doesn't want to see
and maybe, that's why you're dead?

Another candle out, just like the rest
good ones, worth saving
from this godforsaken mess
and I'm here watching just like the rest
of the poor souls left blind
when he took you instead

too much

I play too much about
not caring so much
of the future
of us
whether our lust
could be love
it must
but, I don't care cause
love is too much
melting and learning
leaning and holding
waking next to you
every morning
it's too much

The bottom

deep inside, when I get to thinking
is the bottom of the ocean
where I'm sinking
It is stranger than them
the ones I don't know
like a boss, I don't know
deep inside, far below
is scary because
it's a world where
I'm all alone.
the bottom of bottoms
the bottom I know.

this hell

this town is something
like a jail without cells
where inmates can leave
but they choose to stay
in hell
broken glass on the floor
fundless schools with no doors
a place I adore
a hell I've endured

Please Love Me Forever

Let me forget about today until tomorrow
Let me chase bliss as I run from my sorrow
Let me follow my heart, toward something
unknown
Somewhere more bright
Somewhere like home
Let me laugh uncontrolled, untamed like my
soul
Let me love with heart before the bitterness
turns it cold
Let me, please.
Let me Love.
Let, Me
Live forever.

www.ingramcontent.com/pod-product-compliance
Lightning Source LLC
LaVergne TN
LVHW050250200726
843509LV00015B/2969